How Animals HEAR

Cavendish Square

New York

Joanne Mattern

Library of Congress Cataloging-in-Publication Data

Names: Mattern, Joanne, 1963- author.
Title: How animals hear / Joanne Mattern.
Description: First edition. | New York : Cavendish Square, 2019. | Series: The science of senses | Audience: Grades 2-5. | Includes index Identifiers: LCCN 2018021949 (print) | LCCN 2018023033 (ebook) | ISBN 9781502642035 (ebook) | ISBN 9781502642028 (library bound) | ISBN 9781502642004 (paperback) | ISBN 9781502642011 (6 pack)
Subjects: LCSH: Hearing--Juvenile literature. | Senses and sensation--Juvenile literature. | Animals--Juvenile literature. Classification: LCC QP462.2 (ebook) | LCC QP462.2 .M376 2019 (print) | DDC 612.8/5--dc23
LC record available at https://lccn.loc.gov/2018021949

Editorial Director: David McNamara
Editor: Kristen Susienka
Copy Editor: Nathan Heidelberger
Associate Art Director: Alan Sliwinski
Designer: Ginny Kemmerer
Production Coordinator: Karol Szymczuk
Photo Research: J8 Media

The photographs in this book are used by permission and through the courtesy of: Cover Cherry-Hai/Shutterstock.com; p. 4 AG1100/Shutterstock.com; p. 7 Anup Shah/The Image Bank/Getty Images; p. 8 Sandy Moss Photography/iStock/Thinkstock.com; p. 9 Eddie Dean/Shutterstock.com; p. 10 (top) Tim Davis/Corbis/VCG/Getty Images, (bottom) Vkilikov/Shutterstock.com; p. 11 (top) Saiko3S/Shutterstock.com, (bottom) Jeroen Meeuwsen/Shutterstock.com; p. 12 Jenny Cottingham/Shutterstock.com; p. 15 Paula French/Shutterstock.com; p. 16 Dan Williams Photography/Shutterstock.com; p. 17 Mary Swift/Shutterstock.com; p. 18, 18 Rudmer Zwerver/Shutterstock.com; p. 20 Vladimir Gjorgiev/Shutterstock.com; p. 23 Monika Wisniewska/Shutterstock.com; p. 24 Jack Vanden Heuvel/iStockphoto.com; p. 25 Ronald Wittek/Shutterstock.com; p. 27 Redfox1980/Shutterstock.com.

Printed in the United States of America

CONTENTS

The sound of a refrigerator door opening alerts both people and pets that it is time to eat.

Chapter One

The Science of Hearing

Sounds are all around us. They tell us what is happening in our world. When you hear your friends' voices, you know they are coming to hang out with you. You can talk to them because you hear the words they say and they can hear you. If you hear someone opening the refrigerator, you know it is time for a snack. The sound of a car coming alerts you that you have to wait to cross the street. The blare of the fire alarm at school tells you that you have to leave the building.

Why Hearing Is Important

Hearing is an important sense for animals too. Just like people, animals use the sense of hearing in many ways. They use hearing to communicate, to find food, and to stay safe.

Hearing can tell animals if a **predator** is close. A mouse might hear the cry of a hawk and hurry to safety. A herd of zebras might hear a crackle in the grass and know that a lion is coming toward them.

On the other hand, hearing helps animals find **prey** to eat. An owl has very good hearing. It can hear the quiet sounds of a mouse in the grass far below. A bat listens for **sound waves** that bounce off objects. This

These zebras are running away because they heard a sound that told them danger is near.

tells the bat when an insect is close enough to catch and eat.

Hearing also helps animals communicate. Cats meow and dogs bark to send messages to others. Wolves gather in groups, called packs, and howl. Birds sing songs to attract **mates**.

An owl turns its head so its ear is closer to the ground to hear prey better.

Ears and Other Body Parts

Just like people, most animals have ears. A **mammal** usually has ears on the outside of its head. These ears are shaped to capture sounds. Then the sounds travel to the inner ear.

However, some animals do not have ears on the outside of their bodies. Instead, there might only be a small opening that gathers sounds. Birds and reptiles are two kinds of animals that do not have **external** ears.

FACT!

Grasshoppers have tiny ears on their stomachs.

These animals do have inner ears.

Ears are not the only way animals can hear. Some animals hear through their hair or

Hairs on a jumping spider's body help it feel vibrations that mean prey is near.

their skin. Hairs on a jumping spider's body can feel **vibrations** from far away. **Nerve cells** in these hairs send messages to the brain. This lets the spider hear what is going on. There is a small frog that traps sound waves in its mouth. It sends these waves to its inner ear so it can hear.

Ocean animals do not have external ears. However, they can feel vibrations in the water. These vibrations tell the fish what is nearby. Is it a predator? Is it a ship? Is it something to eat? The fish's sense of hearing lets it know the answer.

ANIMALS AROUND THE WORLD

NORTH AMERICA: Wolves communicate by howling. Hearing these howls tells wolves if other wolves are nearby and what they are doing.

ATLANTIC OCEAN: Dolphins have the best hearing among mammals. They can hear both in the water and when their ears are out of the water. The dolphin's lower jaw can collect sounds and send them to the ears.

ASIA: Pythons and other snakes hear with the help of their lower jaws. Vibrations in the ground travel to the jaw and then to the snake's inner ear.

AFRICA: An elephant has big, wide ears to trap sounds.

A rabbit's big ears help it hear sounds from different directions.

Chapter Two

Hearing in Action

Most mammals have an outer ear and an inner ear. The outer ear collects sound waves. For most animals, sound travels into the outer ear. The vibrations move down a tube called the ear canal. At the end of the ear canal is a thin **membrane** called the eardrum. The sound waves hit the eardrum and make it vibrate. The eardrum vibrates quicker for high-pitched sounds and slower for low-pitched sounds.

Inside the Ear

The vibrating eardrum pushes against small bones inside the ear. These bones send the vibrations to a liquid in the inner ear. The vibrations travel through the liquid until they hit the **cochlea**. The cochlea is shaped like a spiral. It is filled with tiny hairs. The sound waves make these hairs move. That movement sends signals to the brain. The brain changes these signals into sounds.

Different Kinds of Ears

Animal ears come in different sizes. Often, an animal's ears are shaped like cups. This shape helps gather sounds and send them down the ear canal to the inner ear. Some, like a cat's ears, are small. Others, like

A baby elephant's big ears can capture many different sounds.

an elephant's ears, are very large. Some smaller animals have very large ears. A rabbit is a good example of a smaller animal with big ears. These ears pick up lots of sounds. This helps the rabbit stay safe. It is easy for the rabbit to hear danger coming.

Mammals have outer ears, but most other animals do not. For example, many reptiles have eardrums on the sides of their heads. Others have small openings in their heads that lead to eardrums. Eardrums send vibrations to the reptile's inner ear.

A bird has no outer ears. Like some reptiles, it has small holes on the sides of its head. These holes are

FACT!

Most predators on land have ears that face forward.
This helps them hear their prey.

covered with small feathers to protect them. Sound travels into the holes and then to the inner ear. Scientists have studied how birds hear. They know that a bird can tell which direction a sound is coming from by how loud it is. If a sound comes from the right, the bird's ear on its right side will hear the sound louder than the ear on its left side. This information tells the bird exactly where the sound is coming from.

Many insects do not have ears. Instead, other organs pick up vibrations and change

Feathers cover the ear holes on the sides of this owl's head.

them into sounds. For example, some insects have tiny hairs on their bodies that pick up sounds. So do spiders.

What about fish? Fish have bones inside their heads. These bones pick up sounds. They help the fish

This dog might be listening to a sound that is too high for people to hear.

hear. A dolphin has openings on the sides of its head. They help them hear.

High and Low Sounds

Not all sounds are the same. A high-pitched sound has a high **frequency**. That means the sound wave vibrates quickly. Low-pitched sounds vibrate slowly. They have lower frequencies. Some animals can hear different

A mouse's ears can capture tiny sounds and keep the animal safe.

frequencies than people can. Dogs can hear higher frequencies than people.

Hearing sounds at a higher frequency is important for some animals. It allows them to hear more sounds. Hearing sounds can be a matter of life and death. It can help an animal hear a predator. It can help a predator hear prey it wants to eat.

The size of an animal's eardrum and ear bones affects the frequencies it can hear. A thin eardrum vibrates faster than a thick eardrum. This allows an animal like a bat to hear much higher frequencies than a woodchuck. An animal such as a mouse, which has small ear bones, can hear higher frequencies than an elephant, which has large bones.

HEARING THEIR WAY AROUND

Bats use a process called echolocation to find objects. Echolocation works like this: A bat sends out high-pitched squeaks. These squeaks hit nearby objects and

bounce back to the bat's ears as an echo. This tells the bat that something is in front of it.

A bat uses sound waves to find out what is around it as it flies.

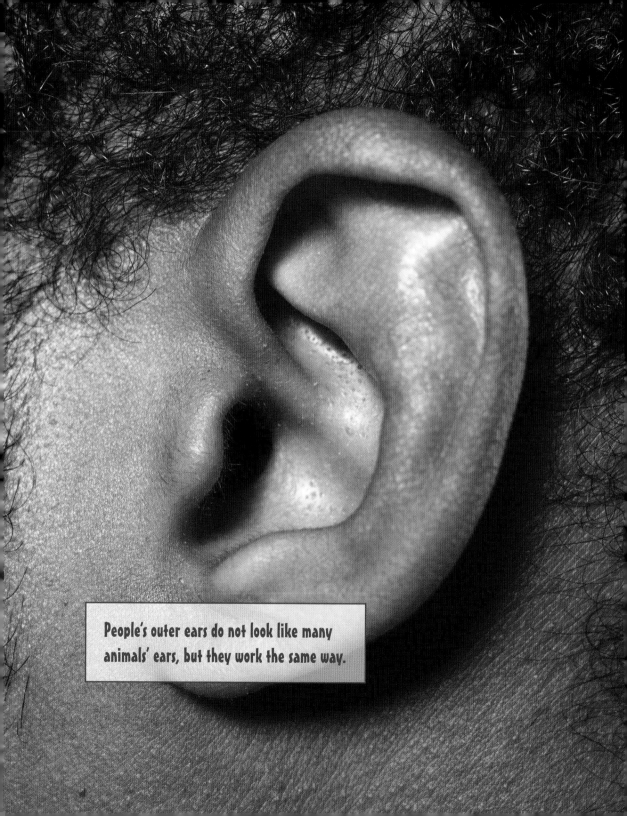

People's outer ears do not look like many animals' ears, but they work the same way.

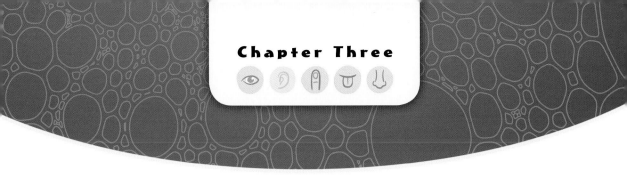

Chapter Three

Hearing the World

People use hearing to learn what is going on around them. Like many animals, humans have an outer ear. The outer ear catches sound waves. The sound waves travel inside the ear. They make the eardrum vibrate. Those vibrations are passed along to the cochlea, which sends them to the brain. The brain tells the person what they hear.

Using Sound

Humans have ears on the sides of their heads. Most humans can't wiggle their ears like a dog, though. Their ears stay in one place. They catch sound and move it to the inner ear.

Hearing can tell people where they are and what is happening. Hearing thunder lets someone know a storm is coming. Hearing voices tells a person others are nearby.

People also use hearing to communicate. We talk and listen to each other. We give each other information

FACT!

A cat has thirty-two muscles in each outer ear. These muscles move the cat's ears in different directions.

or share a funny story. Sometimes we can even tell how a person is feeling by the sound of their voice.

Some people can hear very well. Others need different objects to help them hear. Some people have hearing aids that help them hear better.

Animals and Humans

Animals use hearing in the same ways that people do. Just like people use hearing to know what is happening,

Hearing aids make sounds louder for people who cannot hear well.

animals also use this sense to learn what is going on. A cheetah listens for the sound of a gazelle. The sound tells the cheetah its prey is near. Animals hear storms coming or people approaching. These sounds help animals decide if they are safe or if they need to take shelter.

Communication

The high-pitched chirps of her babies tell this mother robin that her chicks are hungry.

Animals also use sound to communicate. Cats purr and meow to tell each other—and people—how they feel. A mother bird hears her babies' cries in the nest and knows they are hungry.

Communication also helps animals stay safe. For example, meerkats live in large groups. During the day, these animals come outside and dig up insects to eat. Some of the meerkats don't eat. Instead, they act as guards. They look for birds or other predators.

If the guard meerkat hears or sees danger, it chirps loudly. The other meerkats hear the chirp and know they must find safety. In a flash, the whole group disappears into their homes underground. Without the guard chirping to alert them, the animals would become prey.

A group of meerkats stands alert, listening for the sounds of predators.

FACT!

Greater wax moths can hear higher frequencies than any other animal in the world.

Hearing the Way

Hearing is one of the most important senses. It lets humans and animals sense danger, find food, and communicate with each other. The sense of hearing links them to the world.

TOO MUCH NOISE

This bird has built a nest in a traffic light, despite the noise of the cars passing below.

Scientists have studied the effect of noise on animals. They have found that too much noise can cause stress and poor health in wild animals. Animals are especially affected by noise from cars and other sounds made by people. Birds are especially sensitive to noise.

GLOSSARY

cochlea A space in the inner ear that changes vibrations into signals for the brain.

external Outside the body.

frequency The rate at which a sound wave vibrates. The higher the frequency, the higher the pitch of the sound.

mammal A warm-blooded animal that has a backbone and hair, and gives birth to live young.

mates Pairs of animals.

membrane A thin, stretchy sheet of tissue.

nerve cells Special cells that send messages to the brain.

predator An animal that hunts other animals for food.

prey Animals that are eaten for food.

sound waves Repeated waves that move sound through the air, water, or the ground.

vibrations Constant movement.

FIND OUT MORE

Books

Markle, Sandra. *What If You Had Animal Ears?* New York: Scholastic, 2016.

McAneney, Caitie. *How Elephants and Other Animals Hear the Earth.* New York: PowerKids Press, 2016.

Websites

How Do Different Animals Hear?

http://www.funkidslive.com/learn/hallux/hearing/different-animals-hear-ears-like-animals

This website describes how different animals hear and use sounds.

What Animals Have the Biggest Ears in the World?

http://animals.mom.me/animal-biggest-ears-world-2688.html

Take a look at animals that have big ears and learn how these ears help them.

Why Do Some Animals Hear Noises That Others Cannot?

http://animals.mom.me/can-animals-hear-noises-others-cannot-5888.html

This website talks about different frequencies and why some animals hear differently than others.

Videos

Echolocation

https://www.youtube.com/watch?v=laeE4icRYp4

This animated video shows how bats use echolocation to find prey.

How Do Animals Hear?

https://www.youtube.com/watch?v=EowcFKQPYcI

Learn the many different ways animals hear sounds in this lively video.

INDEX

Page numbers in **boldface** are illustrations. Entries in **boldface** are glossary terms.

ABOUT THE AUTHOR

Joanne Mattern is the author of hundreds of nonfiction books for children and young adults. Animals are her favorite subjects to write about, along with sports, history, and biography. Mattern lives in New York State with her husband, children, and an assortment of pets.